# Keys
# to the
# Kingdom

by
**Betty Miller**

First Edition Published 1980
Second Printing 1982
Third Printing 1983
Fourth Printing 1984
Fifth Printing 1987
Sixth Printing 1988
Seventh Printing 1989
Eighth Printing 1991
Ninth Printing 1994
Tenth Printing 2003
Print On Demand

*Keys to the Kingdom*

ISBN 1-57149-006-X

CHRIST UNLIMITED MINISTRIES, INC.
Pastor R.S. "Bud" Miller - Publisher
P.O. Box 850
Dewey, Arizona 86327
All Rights Reserved

Printed in U.S.A.

Scripture quotations are taken from the King James Version
unless otherwise indicated.

# Contents

Preface ................................................................. v

Foreword ............................................................. vii

Credits & Acknowledgments ............................. viii

Introduction ........................................................ ix

Keys to the Kingdom ........................................... 1

Key of Prayer ...................................................... 3

Methods of Prayer ............................................... 5

Agreement in Prayer ........................................... 7

Principles of Prayer ............................................. 8

Intercessory Prayer ........................................... 12

Prayer in Tongues .............................................. 15

Key of Praise ..................................................... 22

Key of Travail .................................................... 27

Key of Fasting ................................................... 35

Restoration of the Church .................................. 44

Index ................................................................. 47

# Contents

# Preface

Greetings in the name of our Lord Jesus Christ:

I present this book to the body of Christ as the Holy Spirit presented it to me. I challenge you to allow God's Spirit of truth, and the Bible, to test the accuracy of the words within these pages. This book, part of the Overcoming Life Series, is also addressed to all seekers of truth who know not THE CHRIST UNLIMITED, as it would be my privilege to introduce you to Him.

During the early years of the ministry, I struggled to learn how to hear the voice of God. Once, while nervously waiting to speak before a large audience, and not being sure on what subject I should speak, I posed to the Lord in prayer this question: "Lord, what am I going to say to all these people?" In my spirit, I heard Him very clearly reply, "Betty, I was hoping you would not say anything, as I really wanted to speak." Yes, He wants to speak through us, as we yield to His Spirit. Submitting to the Lord and the guidance of the Holy Spirit, I found, was not only possible, but the only way He wants us to minister. **For it is not ye that speak, but the Spirit of your Father which speaketh in you (Matthew 10:20).**

This book is a gift from the Holy Spirit. I take no credit for it. If something within these pages blesses you, enlightens you, brings you closer to the Lord, releases you from fear or bondage, or heals or delivers you, then please lift your voice in praise to the precious Savior of our souls, Jesus Christ our Lord! On the other hand, if you find some of these things difficult to receive, hard to understand, or totally heretical from your viewpoint, would you also look to the Lord and ask Him if it could possibly be the truth? With an open and honest heart, will you ask God to change any pre-conceived ideas, and be free from traditions to receive of Him, His truth? His truth always brings freedom, never bondage. **And ye shall know the truth, and the truth shall make you free (John 8:32).**

In walking with the Lord, I have found we must obey the

things we feel He is speaking to us. In my personal life, I used to be fearful of speaking for the Lord because I was so afraid of missing Him and making mistakes. (He, of course, has now delivered me of all my fears. Praise Him!) He encouraged me not to quit because of mistakes when He spoke these words to me: "Betty, if I receive the glory and praise for all the things that are a blessing to people, I also receive the responsibility for your mistakes, as long as you are striving to please me. I am able to make even those work for your good." **And we know that all things work together for good to them that love God, to them who are the called according to his purpose (Romans 8:28).** We serve a wonderful, loving God, who encourages us to follow and obey Him that we might be blessed, and in turn bless others!

This book was written as an act of obedience to the Lord, whom I dearly love. I consider it an honor to write for Him. Years ago, when I was in prayer, the Lord spoke that I was to write a book, but I never felt it was God's timing, nor did I feel the unction or anointing to begin this work until now. Over the past year God has performed a series of miracles to confirm that it is now His time, and has made the arrangements for this to become a reality.

I pray that this book, along with the Overcoming Life Series, may help you learn to walk closer to our Lord, as He is THE CHRIST UNLIMITED!

I am, by His love,
A handmaiden of the Lord,


Betty Miller
February, 1980


**If any man will do his will, he shall know of the doctrine, whether it be of God, or whether I speak of myself (John 7:17).**

# Foreword

It just seemed natural that I would do the foreword on this book since my wife, Betty, and myself, are "one flesh." God, through the Holy Spirit, has given by revelation to Betty many truths of His Word, which have been set forth in this book.

The Lord spoke to Betty about ten years ago that she was to write a book for Him, and that He would arrange the right time and place to write it. Betty simply took this vision and set it aside until God began to "quicken" her spirit to bring it forth. One morning, very early, Betty awakened, and began to write as the Lord dictated to her. In giving her this small initial portion of the book, He showed her how, by submitting to His Spirit, and completely yielding to Him, He would feed to her the message He wanted to share with the body of Christ. He also revealed how quickly and easily it would be completed. The messages that God has given in this Overcoming Life Series are to all who desire to become "overcomers" and be "conformed to the image of His son" **(Romans 8:29).** Our Lord is not satisfied that a person remains a "babe" in Christ, but longs for each "babe" to grow to maturity. He desires that we should strive to become overcomers, live the overcoming life, and claim the promises of the inheritance of all things that are to be given to the overcomers.

I thank God that He has allowed me to share such close love and companionship with Betty. I know that within her heart she has no personal ambitions, no personal ends to achieve. Betty has simply been doing the will of the Father in the writing of this anointed book. May the Lord bless you with this book, as He has blessed us in being a part of His work.

Yours in Christ,

Pastor R.S. "Bud" Miller

**He that overcometh shall inherit all things; and I will be his God and he shall be my son (Revelation 21:7).**

# Credits & Acknowledgments

## ALL PRAISE AND CREDIT
## GOES TO **THE CHRIST UNLIMITED!**

Truly Christ, the Father, and the Holy Spirit, are to be praised, not only for this book, but for our very lives. His sacrifice on Calvary made it possible to know Him and all the members of God's family.

As with the printing of any book, there are lots of people responsible for the words on these pages, physical words as well as spiritual words. All the people that have ever been a part of my life, all the people that have prayed and supported this ministry, my friends and my family have truly contributed to this work. Special credit should be given to my husband, Bud, whose faithful and loving prayers, encouragement, leadership, and love are a big part of this book. Also, to everyone whose books and articles I've read, to the ministers of the Gospel, whose sermons I've heard, I express my gratitude. For each has contributed, in some measure, to this book. The list is endless, but eternity has the records. So instead of naming individuals on this page and giving them earthly credit, I prefer the Lord Jesus Christ to reward them each as only He can. God bless you all, and may you be surprised as you open up the box that contains your heavenly treasures.

**For the Son of man shall come in the glory of his Father with his angels; and then he shall reward every man according to his works (Matthew 16:27).**

# Introduction

*KEYS TO THE KINGDOM* will show you how to gain authority in God's Kingdom through prayer. This book not only details the many different kinds of prayer but also furnishes the believer with the tools needed to live the overcoming life. Topics that are covered include praying in the spirit, fasting, travailing prayer, praise, intercession and spiritual warfare prayer.

The Holy Spirit has been emphasizing spiritual warfare at the present, but so many believers do not understand this powerful form of prayer. Personal spiritual warfare as well as corporate warfare is discussed.

Many believers have experienced unusual things during their prayer times but have not understood the Holy Spirit's leading and have either quenched the spirit of God or have been fearful they were not hearing God in certain areas so have abandoned the burdens of God. *KEYS TO THE KINGDOM* give the believer understanding in these areas with the scripture to bring light to their new level of prayer.

By applying the principles and methods in this book, you will have a rich prayer life that obtains results for the Kingdom of God.

# Keys to the Kingdom

Matthew 16:19 And I will give unto thee the keys
of the kingdom of heaven...

## Keys to the Kingdom

When Jesus becomes our Lord, we are automatically trans-
ferred from the kingdom of darkness into the kingdom of light.
Colossians 1:12-13 says **Giving thanks unto the Father, which
hath made us meet to be partakers of the inheritance of the
saints in light: Who hath delivered us from the power of darkness, and hath translated us into the kingdom of his dear son.**
Now that we have a new king and live in a new kingdom, we must
understand "kingdom principles" if we are to be victorious Christians. We cannot overcome until we have the keys that unlock the
kingdom of heaven. The Lord never meant for us to wait until we
die to experience heaven but purposed for us to bring heaven to
the earth through the power of His Spirit. **Fear not, little flock;
for it is your Father's good pleasure to give you the kingdom
(Luke 12:32).** We are unable to receive God's healing, provision
and blessing if we do not know the keys the Lord has given us to
accomplish kingdom living. Keys represent authority in the Kingdom of God. That authority is gained by using them. The keys to
the kingdom that will be covered here are prayer, praise, worship,
intercession, travail, and fasting.

Looking at **Matthew 16:16-19**, we find an interesting dia-
logue between the Lord Jesus and Peter, His disciple. Jesus has
just asked Peter who he believed Him to be. His answer was,

**Thou art the Christ, the Son of the living God. And Jesus
answered and said unto him, Blessed art thou, Simon Barjona:
for flesh and blood hath not revealed it unto thee, but my**

1

**Father which is in heaven. And I say also unto thee, That thou art Peter, and upon this rock I will build my church; and the gates of hell shall not prevail against it. And I will give unto thee the keys of the kindgom of heaven: and whatsoever thou shalt bind on earth shall be bound in heaven: and whatsoever thou shalt loose on earth shall be loosed in heaven.** From this Scripture we notice that before we can receive the keys to the kingdom, we must first have the same revelation concerning the Lord that Peter had. We must know Him as the Son of the living God. This truth comes only through the revelation of the Holy Spirit.

Peter was the preacher who, after receiving the infilling of the Holy Spirit along with the other 119 in the upper room, began the building of the Lord's church. The first time he preached after receiving the Holy Spirit, three thousand souls were saved. The building of the Lord began taking shape. We need to understand that the church is not the building on the corner, but rather the members of the body of Christ. We are lively stones in the temple of the Holy Spirit.

**1 Peter 2:5-6, Ye also, as lively stones, are built up a spiritual house, an holy priesthood, to offer up spiritual sacrifices, acceptable to God by Jesus Christ. Wherefore also it is contained in the Scripture, Behold, I lay in Sion a chief corner stone, elect, precious: and he that believeth on him shall not be confounded.**

**1 Corinthians 6:19, What? know ye not that your body is the temple of the Holy Ghost which is in you, which ye have of God, and ye are not your own?**

Anyone who has been "born again" and has the Spirit of Christ dwelling in him is a member of the body of Christ. The true church is not a particular denomination, but rather a living organism of God's people all over the world. The bond that holds the stones together is the love of God in their hearts, and the race, color, nationality, sex or age of the individual does not matter. In Jesus we are one body even though we are members of different local churches. Differing Christian doctrines should not separate

2

us, but we should be bound together by His love and unity until doctrines are purified. Those doctrines that are true will emerge as light, while those that are false will fall away. As Christians, the one thing that we can all agree on is our allegiance to Jesus Christ as our Lord!

The Lord spoke to Peter that He was going to build His church and the gates of hell would not prevail against it. What did he mean by this? We all know that a gate is attached to a fence. So this refers to the fact that Satan has some territory that is fenced in, but we are not to be discouraged. We have been given the power to charge Satan's territory and crash down his gates of hell, and they cannot prevail against us.

For so long the church has only been taught to hold the fort, when instead we should be crashing down the gates of hell and rescuing the captives that Satan has placed in bondage (**Luke 10:17-19**). So many are held captive today and need to be set free. How can the Lord use us to free them if we do not know and use the keys to the kingdom?

## Key of Prayer

One of the first keys to the kingdom is that of prayer. Prayer is the primary means we have to communicate with God. What is prayer? In the Greek the word means "to ask, to desire or request." We must remember that when we come to God asking Him for something, our petition must agree with His Word and be in His will, or He will not hear it. **1 John 5:14-15** states, **And this is the confidence that we have in him, that, if we ask any thing according to his will, he heareth us: And if we know that he hear us, whatsoever we ask, we know that we have the petitions that we desired of him.** The Lord only answers our prayers in accordance with His character. They must always be presented in the same spirit of dependence and submission that marked Jesus' relationship to the Father.

We can never demand of God. So many today are using God's Word and demanding Him to keep His own word. How far we have strayed to demand God to answer! We are to approach Him in love and humility, not as a spoiled child commanding our Father to keep His word. If we are not led astray in this approach to God, the devil tries an opposite method to hinder us. He tells us we are unworthy and that we should not bother God with our problems nor ask foolish things of Him. Both of these extremes are unscriptural. **James 4:2** says, **...ye have not, because ye ask not.** The Lord wants us to ask. He is always ready and willing to supply us with the answers.

He cannot give us the answer right away if it would not be good for us. Maybe it would actually turn us away from Him. **James 4:3** continues, **Ye ask, and receive not, because ye ask amiss, that ye may consume it upon your lusts**. Numerous people are claiming cars, money, businesses, houses and other material things. Yet, in God's mercy, He is not answering these prayers at the time for He knows that to give them their request would mean that they would become so involved with the things of this world that they would soon have no time for Him. They would only consume what they receive upon their own lusts, and it would eventually destroy them. Maturity must precede some of God's gifts.

Some people continue to demand even when God says "no" for the present. If they persist to seek the things of this world, eventually the god of this world (Satan) will supply them with the object of their desires, for he does not mind giving an inch to obtain a mile. God steps back while Satan gives them his goods, but soon leanness comes to their souls. **They soon forgat his works; they waited not for his counsel: But lusted exceedingly in the wilderness, and tempted God in the desert. And he gave them their request; but sent leanness into their soul (Psalm 106:13-15)**. The joy and love for Jesus that they once knew will no longer be evident in their lives as these will have been choked out by the cares of this world. We are told to flee worldly lusts.

Now, the Lord does promise to care for us and provide for our needs, so if we follow Him we know that we shall never lack food, clothing or shelter. Out of the goodness of God's heart, He many times gives us lovely things that we do not deserve, simply as an expression of His love for us. These material things are bestowed upon us when we can handle them without getting our eyes off Him. Their value to us should have no meaning aside from their usefulness while we are on this earth. We should be able to gladly part from all of them at the Master's call. He then can allow us to enjoy these material things for they will hold no sway whatsoever over us. If we are not at this place, then we really have not made a total commitment to God.

## Methods of Prayer

When most of us think of prayer, the most common notion would be that of someone praying with the familiar folded hands and bowed head in a kneeling position. However, prayer can take many forms and has really nothing to do with the position of the body, but rather the position or attitude of the heart. We can be on our knees in our heart without physically being in that position. Let us now look at some of the forms and methods of prayer that are mentioned in the Bible so that we can avail ourselves of them.

One Scriptural form of prayer is praying with our hands lifted up. **1 Timothy 2:8, I will therefore that men pray every where, lifting up holy hands, without wrath and doubting. Psalm 63:4, Thus will I bless thee while I live: I will lift up my hands in thy name.** We should learn to worship and pray at times with hands lifted up. It is symbolic of our complete and unconditional surrender to the Lord. In war when someone surrenders, he lifts his hands up to show that he is no longer going to resist. When we surrender to the Lord, it shows Him we are no longer rebelling against Him, but have finally surrendered to His will. Lifted hands also symbolize our willingness to receive from Him, just as little children come to us with uplifted hands in order to be held. We also raise our hands when we are trying to get someone's attention. In a similar manner, this too is a way to get the attention of God. We can see how meaningful it is to worship the Lord with uplifted hands.

In the Bible we find many other body postures assumed by people while in prayer. Some people bowed their heads, others knelt, some fell prostrate to the ground, and some had their faces turned toward heaven, but all were in an attitude of worship. Even Jesus fell on the ground to pray. **Mark 14:35, And he went forward a little, and fell on the ground, and prayed that, if it were possible, the hour might pass from him.**

Another method of prayer is to anoint with oil as the oil is symbolic of the Holy Spirit ministering to our bodies. **James 5:14-15 says, Is any sick among you? let him call for the elders of the church; and let them pray over him, anointing him with oil in the name of the Lord: And the prayer of faith shall save the sick, and the Lord shall raise him up; and if he have committed sins, they shall be forgiven him.**

The "laying on of hands" is still another Scriptural method employed in the Word of God when people are praying for others. Many people have received healing, the Baptism in the Holy Spirit and been touched of God by this method.

**Matthew 19:13, Then were there brought unto him little children, that he should put his hands on them, and pray... Hebrews 6:2, Of the doctrine of baptisms, and of laying on of hands, and of resurrection of the dead, and of eternal judgment. Acts 8:18-20, And when Simon saw that through laying on of the apostles' hands the Holy Ghost was given, he offered them money, Saying, Give me also this power, that on whomsoever I lay hands, he may receive the Holy Ghost. But Peter said unto him, Thy money perish with thee, because thou hast thought that the gift of God may be purchased with**

**money.** These are some of God's "methods" of prayer, but we must be careful to keep this in mind as the Spirit of God cannot be confined to methods only.

In **Matthew 8** there is an account of a centurion, whose servant was sick, who approached Jesus requesting that he heal him. He simply asked the Lord to speak the Word and he knew his servant would be healed. Jesus said he had not seen this great faith in all Israel. This was a simple asking for and sending of the Word. God is limited by neither time nor space. We can pray wherever we are and God can send the answer to our prayers across the miles.

## Agreement in Prayer

One other Scriptural form of prayer is the "prayer of agreement." Let us look at the Scripture that deals with it because it truly is one of the "keys to the kingdom." While we read these verses let us keep in mind that the main subject of these verses is asking or prayer, not "agreement." **Matthew 18:18-19, Verily I say unto you, Whatsoever ye shall bind on earth shall be bound in heaven: and whatsoever ye shall loose on earth shall be loosed in heaven. Again I say unto you, That if two of you shall agree on earth as touching any thing that they shall ask, it shall be done for them of my Father which is in heaven.** For a clearer understanding of this Scripture let us quote from the Amplified Version of the Bible,

**Truly, I tell you, whatever you forbid and declare to be improper and unlawful on earth must be what is already forbidden in heaven, and whatever you permit and declare proper and lawful on earth must be already permitted in heaven. Again I tell you, if two of you on earth agree (harmonize together, together make a symphony) about -- anything and everything -- whatever they shall ask, it will come to pass and be done for them by My Father in heaven.**

7

Here we can see that our agreement is conditional since it must always be in concord with the Word of God. God has many blessings and promises that belong to us as Christians, but they are not "automatic," and they will only come as we keep the Biblical principles necessary to produce our prayer answers. We cannot "bind" anything on earth that is not "bound" in heaven, or "loose" anything that is not already "loosed" in heaven. So we can see that the aforementioned agreement must be more than two people simply deciding that they want something and then asking for it together. Our prayers must agree with the Word and Spirit of God. We must have both witnesses for them to meet the requirements of valid prayer requests. **Verse 16** of this chapter says, **...that in the mouth of two or three witnesses every word may be established.** A lot of people are agreeing on things that the Word and Spirit of God are not in agreement with and therefore, they are not receiving their answers. We don't just decide to "bind" something or "loose" something arbitrarily, but we must see what the Word of God has "bound" or "loosed," and then pray in accordance with that Word. A general guideline would be to "bind" the works of the devil and "loose" the blessings of God, or we could "bind" hearts in love and command the devil to "loose" his hold.

## Principles of Prayer

An important principle of prayer that needs to be mentioned here is to whom are we to direct our prayers? **John 16:23 says, And in that day ye shall ask me nothing. Verily, verily, I say unto you, Whatsoever ye shall ask the Father in my name, he will give it you.** We see that in our prayers we are to address the Father, in the name of Jesus. Never are we to pray to the Spirit as He abides within. Of course, it is permissible to address the Lord by other names such as Master, God, Jehovah, Righteous King, Immanuel, etc. However, our prayers are to be directed to the Heavenly Father, regardless of the Scriptural name we may use.

We may speak to the Father and Jesus interchangeably as we pray, but the Father is the one who will answer our prayers.

Volumes have been written about prayer and this subject could be an exhaustive one in itself. However, it will suffice for us to mention only a few more things here. Prayerlessness is sin for we are admonished in **1 Thessalonians 5:17** to **Pray without ceasing.** How is this possible? Our petitions to the Lord should be continuous. This can only take place as we bring our thoughts and hearts into a constant attitude of prayer. The Lord desires that we have unbroken fellowship with Him.

We also are not to be discouraged if our prayers are not answered immediately. We are instructed in **Matthew 7:7-8** to: **Keep on asking and it will be given you; keep on seeking and you will find; keep on knocking (reverently) and the door will be opened to you. For every one who keeps on asking receives, and he who keeps on seeking finds, and to him who keeps on knocking it will be opened** (Amp. Bible).

This does not mean we are to beg God for our answers, but we are to be diligent and to persevere until our answers come. We don't have to ask for the same thing over and over as the Lord remembers every prayer we pray. Nevertheless, we can pray many ways about the same problem until it is resolved and we obtain our answer.

There are two extremes that the enemy attempts to put upon people in this area. One is to make them think that it is sin and shows lack of faith to ever mention a request to God a second time. He gets them to refuse to ever ask prayer over a problem after praying once. This erroneous belief opens the door to the enemy in situations where he is hindering prayer answers. It sometimes takes considerable spiritual prayer force applied to a specific problem before its answer comes. The problem needs to be prayed completely through before we cease to ask. The other extreme is to continually ask, beg and be prayed for in every prayer line, over and over. This lets the enemy keep our eyes on our problem instead of on the Lord. There is a balance that needs to be applied as we seek God for our answers. If we have peace about something, then we need not continually ask God about it. If we do not have rest in our heart about it, we need to keep praying until we pray the matter through and get peace about it.

Praying in the Spirit is helpful here, as many times we do not know how to pray about a situation. **1 Corinthians 14:14-15** says, **For if I pray in an unknown tongue, my spirit prayeth, but my understanding is unfruitful. What is it then? I will pray with the spirit, and I will pray with the understanding also: I will sing with the spirit, and I will sing with the understanding also.**

Any teaching on prayer would be incomplete without including the "Lord's Prayer." It is a classic memorized by millions, yet lived by few. **Matthew 6:5-13** covers the principles that the Lord Jesus laid down in regard to prayer:

**And when thou prayest, thou shall not be as the hypocrites are: For they love to pray standing in the synagogues and in the corners of the streets, that they may be seen of men. Verily I say unto you, They have their reward. But thou, when thou prayest, enter into thy closet, and when thou hast shut thy door, pray to thy Father which is in secret; and thy Father which seeth in secret shall reward thee openly. But when ye pray, use not vain repetitions, as the heathen do: for they think that they shall be heard for their much speaking. Be not ye therefore like unto them: for your Father knoweth what things ye have need of, before ye ask him. After this manner therefore pray ye: Our Father which art in heaven, Hallowed be thy name. Thy kingdom come. Thy will be done in earth, as it is in heaven. Give us this day our daily bread. And forgive us our debts, as we forgive our debtors. And lead us not into temptation, but deliver us from evil: For thine is the kingdom, and the power, and the glory, for ever. Amen.**

The most important thing the Lord is stressing here is that our hearts need to be right before Him when we pray. Hypocrites that are praying to be heard by others will not be heard by God.

The reward they receive is the pleasure they derive from being able to be seen and heard of men, yet they have no reward from their heavenly Father. The Lord instructs us to pray from the secret chambers of our hearts; this is what He means by entering into our closets. We are to pray from our hearts to the Father and not pray just to be heard of men.

He also says that the heathens use vain repetitions and we are not to do this. These would be memorized prayers that come from the mind with no "heart" to them. They believe their "much speaking" will get through to God. Hindus and Moslems chant prayers such as these. Some use prayer beads as they rotely repeat the same prayers. God is not as interested in the quantity of our prayers as He is in the quality.

Jesus, in His prayer to the Father, begins with an attitude of worship, then asks that the will of God be done in earth. Notice the words "in earth." We are referred to in **2 Corinthians 4:6-7** as "earthen vessels." **For God, who commanded the light to shine out of darkness, hath shined in our hearts, to give the light of the knowledge of the glory of God in the face of Jesus Christ. But we have this treasure in earthen vessels, that the excellency of the power may be of God, and not of us.** The will of God is to be accomplished "in us" as it is in heaven. Is there any sickness, worry, evil, fear or sin in heaven? Since there is not, then we are not to have these things dwelling in us either.

Then we are to ask for our daily bread, but we need a spiritual supply also. We should receive "fresh manna" from the Lord every day and not live on yesterday's prophecies or words from the Lord.

We are to ask for forgiveness of our sins. Then we are especially to forgive those that have trespassed against us. We can block the receiving of our blessings from God if we do not pray for the forgiveness of those who have wronged us.

We are to daily ask for deliverance from evil. We need to ask the Lord to cleanse us from unrighteousness and deliver us from all that would offend our Father. We can stay ahead of the devil by

11

asking the Lord to "lead us not into temptation." If we aggressively stand against Satan's devised attacks and temptations, then we can thwart his plans before he comes against us. We know that he shall be defeated because our God has the true kingdom, the power, and the glory forever! Amen.

## Intercessory Prayer

The Lord instructed us to pray not only for our needs but to reach out and pray for others as well. We find this in **1 Timothy 2:1-6.**

**I exhort therefore, that, first of all, supplications, prayers, intercessions, and giving of thanks, be made for all men; For kings, and for all that are in authority; that we may lead a quiet and peaceable life in all godliness and honesty. For this is good and acceptable in the sight of God our Savior; Who will have all men to be saved, and to come unto the knowledge of the truth. For there is one God, and one mediator between God and men, the man Christ Jesus; Who gave himself a ransom for all, to be testified in due time.**

We are told to pray and to make intercession for all men. What is intercessory prayer? The Greek noun, "enteuxus," is the word for "intercession." It primarily denotes a "meeting with," a conversation or petition rendered on the behalf of others. "Intercessory prayer," then, is seeking the presence and audience of God in another's stead.

Jesus was the greatest intercessor of all time. **Isaiah 53:12** records the following prophecy about Jesus: **Therefore will I divide him a portion with the great, and he shall divide the spoil with the strong; because he hath poured out his soul unto death: and he was numbered with the transgressors; and he bare the sin of many, and made intercession for the transgressors. Hebrews 7:25** speaks of Him as a high priest that is still interceding on our behalf. **Wherefore he is able also to**

**save them to the uttermost that come unto God by him, seeing he ever liveth to make intercession for them.**

The Lord is looking for men and women today that are willing to enter into this ministry with Him. He has always sought people that would "stand in the gap" for others. **Ezekiel 22:30-31 says,**

**And I sought for a man among them, that should make up the hedge, and stand in the gap before me for the land, that I should not destroy it: but I found none. Therefore have I poured out mine indignation upon them; I have consumed them with the fire of my wrath: their own way have I recompensed upon their heads, saith the Lord God.**

The Lord does not want judgment to fall upon people. He desires that they repent and return to Him. However, if they do not repent, judgment is inevitable. Prayer for others causes them to repent and seek God. Therefore, the Lord is always looking for those who will take a burden of prayer for the wayward ones, so that they might come to Him. He needs spiritual warriors who will selflessly intercede on behalf of others. The ministry of intercessory prayer perennially stands open for volunteers who will join the Lord in this work. Through this ministry one can circle the entire world interposing for the multitudes who have no one else to "stand in the gap" for them. I personally do not believe the Lord will call anyone into a public ministry unless the ministry of intercession has first become a priority in his life. There are many people eagerly wanting to do something for Jesus while this important field of work stands wide open. It is certainly not as glamorous as some other ministries, for no one is seen or applauded in their prayer closet, and perhaps that is exactly why there are so few volunteers. Even when people are interested in serving in this form of ministry, there is often a lack of knowledge as to the equipment and the keys needed to be effective and successful in it.

Some of these keys are presented here in hopes that if you have a heart toward God and are willing to become an intercessor, you will know how to obtain many victories. Intercessory prayer, being a ministry to others, is not something that directly benefits us. It is essentially an outreach ministry. Through it we can truly lay down our lives for others. As we are faithful by sacrificing our time on the behalf of others, the Lord then takes care of our needs. As we minister to others, the Lord ministers to us. While praying for others, we cannot neglect mentioning the added blessing of being in fellowship with the Lord. As the Holy Spirit directs us in the ways we are to pray for others, we need to keep in mind that He will always have us pray according to His Word.

Negative prayers and judgment prayed down on people are not in harmony with the Spirit of the Lord. God is continually extending mercy and help. Some people in ignorance pray for God to do whatever it takes to save someone. They pray such prayers as, "Lord, if you have to break their back to get them to come to you, break their back Jesus, take their business away from them, but save them. God, if it takes a car wreck to save them, do it Lord. Show them, even if they have to get cancer." These are examples of the way some ignorant Christians pray. They are truly crimes against the heart of Christ. He came to save, not to destroy and kill.

**Luke 9:53-56, And they did not receive him, because his face was as though he would go to Jerusalem. And when his disciples James and John saw this, they said, Lord, wilt thou that we command fire to come down from heaven, and consume them, even as Elias did? But he turned, and rebuked them, and said, Ye know not what manner of spirit ye are of. For the Son of man is not come to destroy men's lives, but to save them. And they went to another village.** No one gets saved just because he gets cancer. If that were true, then every one that had cancer would automatically come to God. Getting cancer, or being in a car wreck, never saved anyone. On the other hand, many people have died and gone to hell in these ways. Granted, some do come to the Lord when tragedy strikes, but it was the strength of someone praying for them and the mercy of the Holy

Spirit that caused them to come to God, not the tragedy. Without the conviction of the Holy Spirit, their thoughts would never have gone out to God even in their crisis.

God does not send calamities in order to bring people to Himself. He tells us in His word that it is the Spirit of God that "woos" and "draws" people to Himself. This is hastened as Christians pray. **John 6:44** says, **No man can come to me, except the Father which hath sent me draw him: and I will raise him up at the last day.** Praise God for intercessors that stand against the enemy and keep him from destroying the souls and lives of men, women and children who need the Lord.

The ministry of intercession is a vital part of our Christian walk and we can never attain to maturity and become overcomers by slighting it. I often use the words "task" and "work" in reference to prayer because it is never easy nor convenient to pray with any discipline or consistency. We must remember that we have an enemy (the devil) who is constantly trying to keep us from our prayer life because he knows (better than most Christians) the damage done to his kingdom through it. Let us never cease to pray.

## Prayer in Tongues

One tremendous weapon that is available to us as Christians is a form of prayer that has caused much controversy in the body of Christ. Even so, it should not be left out because it is definitely one of the keys to the kingdom. This valuable type of prayer is praying in an unknown tongue or praying in the spirit. Paul declares in **1 Corinthians 14:14-15**,

**For if I pray in an unknown tongue, my spirit prayeth, but my understanding is unfruitful. What is it then? I will pray with the spirit, and I will pray with the understanding also: I will sing with the spirit, and I will sing with the understanding also.**

15

Due to the commotion that "tongues" has raised in the body of Christ, many people would just as soon do away with it. Yet, there have been many other issues within the church which have caused problems that have not been put aside simply because they created discord. We must resolve the contention, not throw out speaking in tongues. The Bible has to remain the standard of truth. We cannot eliminate portions of it just because we do not understand it all.

Paul wrote a letter to the Corinthians because they were having problems in the church, including the same one we are having today regarding speaking in tongues (see **I Corinthians 14**). Nowhere in this chapter does Paul recommend doing away with this gift of the Holy Spirit; instead he deals with correcting the problem. Most of the problems regarding speaking in tongues stem from a lack of understanding of what the purpose of this beautiful gift is.

Let us look at this entire chapter to clear up the confusion. Verse 1 begins:

**Follow after charity, and desire spiritual gifts, but rather that ye may prophesy. For he that speaketh in an unknown tongue speaketh not unto men, but unto God: for no man understandeth him; howbeit in the spirit he speaketh mysteries**.

From this we can see that when one speaks in tongues, he is not speaking to men, but to God. We need to understand this because many people do not see any purpose for speaking in tongues, and therefore do not see their need for this gift. They contend that love is the only thing in a Christian's life. We find two main groups, one emphasizing on the gifts, and the other the fruit of the Spirit. The truth is, however, that it is necessary to possess both. It takes "two wings for a bird to fly."

The words of the Lord Jesus, just before his ascension to heaven (after His resurrection), have been called the "Great Commission" to the church. The fulfillment of the Great Commission

16

requires both the fruit and the gifts. This account is recorded in **Mark 16:15-20:**

**And he said unto them, Go ye into all the world, and preach the gospel to every creature. He that believeth and is baptized shall be saved; but he that believeth not shall be damned. And these signs shall follow them that believe; In my name shall they cast out devils; they shall speak with new tongues; They shall take up serpents; and if they drink any deadly thing, it shall not hurt them; they shall lay hands on the sick, and they shall recover. So then after the Lord had spoken unto them, he was received up into heaven, and sat on the right hand of God. And they went forth, and preached every where, the Lord working with them, and confirming the word with signs following. Amen.**

People's last words before departing have always been considered important. Here our Lord's words tell us that we are to take the gospel to every creature that they might believe, be saved, and be baptized. He does not stop with the salvation message, but goes on to instruct His disciples that they should cast out demons, speak with new tongues, heal the sick, and that nothing would have any power over them, not even poison. He said these signs would follow "them that believe." He did not say just the apostles would do these things, but all who were believers.

If this message had been intended only for the apostles, then why are we still preaching the gospel today? Either the entire commission was only for the apostles, or it was for all believers. Today, our churches split this commission, as they are strong on preaching the gospel, teaching that it is the duty of every Christian to witness to others, yet ignoring the other half, that of speaking with tongues, healing the sick and casting out demons. They have been teaching only half a gospel instead of the "full gospel." Today, the Lord wants the same signs that followed the early day believers to follow us. It is a confirmation that He is with us when we have these signs evident in our lives.

On several missionary journeys, we have had opportunity

17

for a portion of this Scripture to become very real to us. Some of the food and drink we consumed might have been deadly to us, but the Lord sanctified it and we did not suffer sickness which could have come had we not had faith in His Word. It was quite a struggle for me, with my medical background, to maintain my trust in the Lord, for I knew just what microorganisms were rampant especially in foreign lands. However, we knew God had sent us on His mission; and just as He told His disciples to eat and drink what was set before them and that nothing by any means would harm them, we knew that His Word was just as true and reliable today as it was then.

**Luke 10:8-9, And into whatsoever city ye enter, and they receive you, eat such things as are set before you: And heal the sick that are therein, and say unto them, The Kingdom of God is come nigh unto you. Luke 10:19, Behold, I give unto you power to tread on serpents and scorpions, and over all the power of the enemy: and nothing shall by any means hurt you. Hebrews 13:8, Jesus Christ the same yesterday, and today, and for ever.**

Of course, there are always extremists who pervert the Scripture. Thus, we have some occult groups today who actually handle poisonous serpents in their rituals. This was certainly not the Lord's meaning here. He is saying that if a serpent should bite us, or we should (not knowingly) drink poison, it will not harm us. Paul experienced the truth of this while on the island Melita. **Act 28:3-5** records,

**And when Paul had gathered a bundle of sticks, and laid them on the fire, there came a viper out of the heat, and fastened on his hand. And when the barbarians saw the venomous beast hang on his hand, they said among themselves, No doubt this man is a murderer, whom, though he hath escaped the sea, yet vengeance suffereth not to live. And he shook off the beast into the fire, and felt no harm.** A parallel meaning to the Scripture is that we shall also have this same power and invulnerability over Satan and his demons, as he is referred to as "the old serpent," the devil.

**Luke 10:17-19, And the seventy returned again with joy, saying, Lord, even the devils are subject unto us through thy name. And he said unto them, I beheld Satan as lightning fall from heaven. Behold, I give unto you power to tread on serpents and scorpions, and over all the power of the enemy: and nothing shall by any means hurt you.**

The Lord does not send us out to do His work without His power and His gifts.

The gift of tongues is an important part of our prayer life as it gives us that power and prepares us for spiritual battles, enabling us to pray as the Spirit directs instead of being solely dependent on our natural minds and understanding. While praying in the Spirit, we not only speak mysteries unto God, but also we pray according to His will. **Romans 8:27** says, **And he that searcheth the hearts knoweth what is the mind of the Spirit, because he maketh intercession for the saints according to the will of God.** The Spirit of God directs our spirit how to pray when we pray in tongues. This is a wonderful blessing, particularly when we do not know exactly how to pray about a situation.

We do not understand why God chose this method of prayer, but as with other things in God's Word that we do not understand with the natural mind, they remain truths none the less. When I was seeking this particular gift, one of my objections was that I could not see why we needed to speak in a language that we did not understand. The Lord spoke to my heart and asked me if I understood the mysteries of salvation. I replied, "No." He then said, "But you accepted salvation, received Me in your heart, and were saved even though you did not understand why Jesus had to die on a cross for your sins." I replied, "Yes." He said, "It is the same way with the Holy Spirit and speaking in tongues; if you will ask for this blessing you will receive Him, and He will give you a heavenly language with which to pray and worship. You'll find

19

that you will have joy, peace, love and power in a new dimension."

Speaking in tongues is also given to build us up. **1 Corinthians 14:3-4** states, **But he that prophesieth speaketh unto men to edification, and exhortation, and comfort. He that speaketh in an unknown tongue edifieth himself; but he that prophesieth edifieth the church.** The word edify means to "build up;" therefore, praying in tongues strengthens us and lifts our spirits while the gift of prophecy strengthens and builds up the church. When we pray in tongues, we get blessed. We pray about whatever our number one problem and need is. The Holy Spirit knows better than we what our needs are. For example, we do not know what is ahead of us each day, but the Lord does. If He saw an attack of the enemy coming, He could prompt us to pray in the spirit to offset the devil's attack. The Lord knows every test, trial or attack that is coming up, and desires to see us prepared to meet and overcome it by implementing this valuable tool of praying in tongues. It is hard for us to reach out to others when we are burdened ourselves, so praying in the spirit about our problems also frees us to then intercede for others.

We can also use our unknown tongue to pray and intercede for others. It is truly a powerful weapon against the devil. That is why the devil tries so hard to keep people from asking for it. He even lies and says the gift of tongues is from him, just to keep people from receiving it and using it against him.

True, there are false gifts of tongues from the devil, and several occult groups practice them. Satan always tries to counterfeit the real thing. However, these false tongues do not edify and are really more of a chant. A typical example would be the "mantra" in Transcendental Meditation. These tongues are inspired by the devil, not the Holy Spirit. We never need fear receiving anything false from the Lord if we are seeking our gift from Him. **Luke 11:11-13** gives us that assurance:

If a son shall ask bread of any of you that is a father, will he give him a stone? or if he ask a fish, will he for a fish give him a serpent? Or if he shall ask an egg, will he offer him a scorpion? If ye then, being evil, know how to give good gifts unto your children: how much more shall your heavenly Father give the Holy Spirit to them that ask him?

Throughout **Chapter 14 of 1 Corinthians** Paul encourages us to pray in tongues, and pray with our understanding. In **verse 18** he says, **I thank my God, I speak with tongues more than ye all.** In **verse 21**, Paul quotes a verse from **Isaiah 28:11, For with stammering lips and another tongue will he speak to this people.** Sometimes people receive a beautiful tongue in a foreign sounding language, while others only receive stammering syllables or a few strange words. Do not be discouraged at whatever sound comes out. It is beautiful to God and it comes from His Spirit.

Paul tells us in **verse 5, I would that ye all spake with tongues, but rather that ye prophesied: for greater is he that prophesieth than he that speaketh with tongues, except he interpret, that the church may receive edifying.** Speaking in tongues edifies us, but it does not edify someone else unless there is an interpretation.

A lack of understanding causes confusion, as people do not realize that there are two kinds of speaking in tongues, One type is given to all who desire it and are baptized in His Spirit; the other is a ministry gift mentioned in **1 Corinthians 12:30**. In this verse the question is asked, **Do all speak with tongues?** This is not speaking about the tongues available to all, but refers to those Christians called to minister in tongues before the church. This ministry of tongues is coupled with the ministry of interpretation, so that the whole church can be edified. The individual gift of tongues is indeed a priceless key that unlocks many of the doors that hinder our walk with the Lord. If we are to walk in victory we need to seek the Lord and ask Him not only for this gift, but for all that is available to us as His children.

## Key of Praise

Another key that will make it possible for us to walk in kingdom living is our expression of praise. The Lord's prayer begins in an attitude of worship and praise, **Our Father which art in heaven, Hallowed be thy name. Thy kingdom come. Thy will be done, as in heaven, so in earth (Luke 11:2)**. Praise is the will of God, and heaven overflows with it.

**And a voice came out of the throne, saying, Praise our God, all ye his servants, and ye that fear him, both small and great. And I heard as it were the voice of a great multitude, and as the voice of many waters, and as the voice of mighty thunderings, saying, Alleluia: for the Lord God omnipotent reigneth. Let us be glad and rejoice, and give honor to him: for the marriage of the Lamb is come, and his wife hath made herself ready (Revelation 19:5-7).**

Since the presence of praise is voiced continually in heaven, our voices should also be lifted up in praise to our Lord. In **1 Thessalonians 5:16-18** we are told to, **Rejoice evermore. Pray without ceasing. In every thing give thanks: for this is the will of God in Christ Jesus concerning you.** The Lord tells us here that we are to have an attitude of joy, thanksgiving and prayer at all times, no matter what the conditions or circumstances are that surround us.

This verse does not mean that we are to thank God for bad things and tragedies that come our way. It means that we are to remain joyful no matter what is happening in our lives because we have the Lord, and in Him we shall overcome no matter what the devil is trying to do to us. The Lord does not want us to thank Him for the bad things that happen to us because He did not send them. He is not the author of evil. We are not to become bitter over life's circumstances, but rather to continue to rejoice in the Lord. It is the will of God for us to rejoice no matter what comes. It is not the will of God to receive evil things as from Him. It is an insult to God to thank Him for accidents, sickness, tragedy, etc. He does not send those things to us, the devil does. We are told to resist the devil, and submit to God. **(James 4:7, Submit yourselves therefore to God. Resist the devil, and he will flee from you.)** We are to love and rejoice in the Lord in spite of what the devil tries to do to us.

One of Satan's favorite schemes is to send something bad into someone's life and blame it on God. If he can get people to believe it is from the Lord, he has an easier time convincing them of his next lie, that God has failed them and deserted them. He follows this up with a further lie, "Why go on serving a God who does these kinds of things to you?" Satan's real target is to destroy our faith in God. He just attacks different areas to get at different people.

Our prayers should be in an attitude of praise even in the midst of our trials. We should lift our voices and praise the Lord like this, "Father, I praise You and love You, and no matter what the devil is doing to me I know that You shall bring me through victoriously! Show me what I need to do, Lord. Show me the door that I have opened to the enemy. I resist him in the name of Jesus, and I command him to leave with all of his oppression and attacks. Jesus, You are the Lord of my life, and I submit to You and will never deny You no matter what happens. Praise God!".

Instead of praying like that, many Christians fall for the enemy's lies and come under condemnation and suffering. They begin to question God and even become mad at Him. The fault is not the Lord's but our own. We miss His complete victory because we have attributed Satan's attack to the Lord. We can even open the door for the enemy to come against us by not having a cheerful and rejoicing heart. We may complain and gripe to God about our plight in life instead of using the weapons He has given

23

us to overcome the devil. One of the greatest weapons is our weapon of praise.

David in writing the Psalms expresses many praises to the Lord. **Psalm 34** is a typical psalm of praise:

**I will bless the Lord at all times: his praise shall continually be in my mouth. My soul shall make her boast in the Lord: the humble shall hear thereof, and be glad. O magnify the Lord with me, and let us exalt his name together. I sought the Lord, and he heard me, and delivered me from all my fears**.

We are to bless God at all times, not just when things go smoothly. We are to bless Him when things go wrong, too. We are to boast in the Lord even when all looks bleak. Our prayer should be similar to David's "Father, I love and appreciate You. I know You are going to bring the answer I need because You are a good God, and You care for me. I trust You, Lord, no matter what I see with my natural eyes. I am looking through the eyes of faith, and I believe You are sending my answer. I love You, Lord, no matter what happens." When we keep this attitude of praise in the midst of our trials, we come through victoriously.

Praising God when we do not feel like praising Him is called a sacrifice of praise. **Hebrews 13:15** says, **By him therefore let us offer the sacrifice of praise to God continually, that is, the fruit of our lips giving thanks to his name.** Feelings fall into the emotional and soulish realm of our being. If we wait until we feel like praising God, we may never do it. Our spirits desire to praise God because of His nature in us. However, the soulish part of us resists that desire, until our carnal minds have been completely renewed in this area. That is why it is important to go ahead and praise God to a point beyond our soulish feelings until we press on into the spirit. We will then sense a real joy, and praise will come forth. **Psalm 103** is a wonderful praise psalm:

**Bless the Lord, O my soul: and all that is within me, bless his holy name. Bless the Lord, O my soul, and forget not all his benefits: Who forgiveth all thine iniquities; who healeth**

all thy diseases; Who redeemeth thy life from destruction; who crowneth thee with loving-kindness and tender mercies; Who satisfieth thy mouth with good things; so that thy youth is renewed like the eagle's. The Lord executeth righteousness and judgment for all that are oppressed.

David is saying, "Soul, you are going to bless the Lord regardless of whether you feel like it or not." If we would begin our praises in the natural, they would soon end up in the Spirit, even as David said that all that was within him would bless the Lord. What kind of benefits do we receive from the Lord? He forgives our sins, heals all our diseases, shows us His love and kindness, is merciful toward us, gives us good things to eat, restores our youth and strength, delivers us from oppression and judges us righteously. We have so much to praise God about because He is a wonderful and loving Father!

Praise is a wonderful method we can use to bring healing and deliverance to our souls and bodies! Many people are depressed today; one of the quickest ways to receive deliverance from depression is to praise God. We must make our souls bless the Lord when we are not feeling well. It will bring liberation and healing.

Psalm 30:1-4, I will extol thee, O Lord; for thou hast lifted me up, and hast not made my foes to rejoice over me. O Lord my God, I cried unto thee, and thou hast healed me. O Lord, thou hast brought up my soul from the grave: thou hast kept me alive, that I should not go down to the pit. Sing unto the Lord, O ye saints of his, and give thanks at the remembrance of his holiness.

Singing unto the Lord also can bring quick relief from despondence and oppression. We all feel like we are in the "pits" when that horrible sensation of apathy comes over us. Singing praises can bring us up out of that pit. Music plays an important part in a worship service and we have all experienced how our hearts have been lifted by singing and worshiping in church. We do not have to wait until we go to a service to receive this same benefit. We can worship out of our hearts wherever we are.

In the Old Testament there is an account of a battle that was won by God's people simply as a group of appointed singers went before the army as it marched toward battle. They sang and praised God, and the Lord did their battling for them. They won the battle without a sword even being drawn.

**2 Chronicles 20:21-22: And when he had consulted with the people, he appointed singers unto the Lord, and that should praise the beauty of holiness, as they went out before the army, and to say, Praise the Lord; for his mercy endureth forever. And when they began to sing and to praise, the Lord set ambushments against the children of Ammon, Moab, and mount Seir, which were come against Judah; and they were smitten.**

Our battles can also be won through praise.

In **Psalm 22:3** the word declares that God himself inhabits the praises of His people: **But thou art holy, O thou that inhabitest the praises of Israel**. As we sing and praise God, we begin to feel the presence of the Lord upon us. It can also be helpful to listen to gospel music when we are fighting a spiritual battle. It will liberate our spirits, too. When we praise and bless God, we find that other people around us respond to that spirit of praise also. Conversely, when we complain and grumble, we exude that kind of spirit and drive people away from us because no one wants to be around a pessimist. Lonely people filled with self-pity have not found the key of praise in their lives. They lack the joy of the Lord and do not make good companions. As we rejoice in God, we spread a spirit of joy to others. If we complain about things, it works against us. No one wants to be around someone who causes them also to get into a bad mood. Let us all bless and praise God and conquer the enemy in this important area.

The overcomers in the book of Revelation are praisers, and they sing a new song before the throne. The hundred forty-four thousand seen here are representatives of the tribes of Israel. One

26

of these tribes is the tribe of Judah. The name Judah means "praise." We can clearly see that one of the attributes of the hundred forty-four thousand is an attitude of praise (**Revelation 7 and 14**). Praise is a heavenly characteristic, and if we are to be overcomers, we too will strive to possess this quality.

## Key of Travail

A key that might sound contradictory after discussing praise is the key of travailing prayer. What is travailing prayer? It is crying in the Spirit which can take on several different manifestations. Before discussing this let us look at the Bible definition found in **John 16:20-22,**

**Verily, verily, I say unto you, That ye shall weep and lament, but the world shall rejoice: and ye shall be sorrowful, but your sorrow shall be turned into joy. A woman when she is in travail hath sorrow, because her hour is come: but as soon as she is delivered of the child, she remembereth no more the anguish, for joy that a man is born into the world. And ye now therefore have sorrow: but I will see you again, and your heart shall rejoice, and your joy no man taketh from you.**

Jesus, speaking here to his disciples, leaves them with a beautiful promise. He tells them He is going away, but He is not going to leave them comfortless as He plans to send the Holy Spirit. They later will cry at His departure, yet when they experience the new birth and the infilling of the Holy Spirit, they will rejoice.

Travailing prayer is a manifestation of the grief of the heart of God. This also has a parallel meaning when applied to prayer that cries out unto God. Perhaps we can understand this better if we realize that we now have the Holy Spirit living in us, and He has chosen to use our mouths to speak for Him. Since He has chosen to use us in His great plan to spread the gospel, He uses our mouths to witness to others and our hands to help people. Another beautiful truth that is often overlooked is that He also uses our hearts and emotions to weep and "cry through." The Spirit of God expresses His grief in this manner.

Most Christians have experienced this without ever realizing it was a work of the Holy Spirit. At their conversion they sometimes wept and cried, grieved over their sins. Then later they got a burden for the salvation and deliverance of others, and cried over them also. This is known as travailing prayer. When we have a burden for others and become sorrowful over them, it is usually the Holy Spirit crying through us over the situation.

There is another kind of weeping and crying, but it is in the flesh and stems from our own selfishness as it is from self-pity. Fleshly crying is always concerned over self. Crying in the Spirit is Godly sorrow for others. **(2 Corinthians 7:10, For godly sorrow worketh repentance to salvation not to be repented of: but the sorrow of the world worketh death.)** If we cry in self-pity it brings depression and fear; but crying in the Spirit brings life and joy after it is finished, just as a woman cries to bring forth a child during labor, yet she is rejoices as soon as the child is born.

We do the same as we yield to the Spirit and take prayer burdens for others. God's heart is burdened for people, and He is looking for hearts that He can cry and weep through, hearts that are concerned for a lost and dying world. So, in essence, travailing prayer is when we weep and cry over something the Holy Spirit is grieved about. Jesus said they would weep and cry for a little while, but then their sorrow would be turned into joy.

Travailing prayer works on the same principle. We do not understand all the principles in God's word, nor why they work, but because they are a part of His plan, they work. This neglected principle and key is of vital importance in order to see things "born" in the Spirit. When we weep and cry over others while we petition God on their behalf, it breaks something in the Spirit so that the answer for their lives can come forth. If they need salvation, healing, a miracle, deliverance or whatever, grieving in the Spirit releases them to be able to receive their need. **(Psalm 126:5-6, They** that sow in tears shall reap in joy. He that goeth forth and weepeth, bearing precious seed, shall doubtless come again with rejoicing, bringing his sheaves with him.)

Sometimes this spirit of travail does not manifest with visible tears or crying, but it occurs deep within us and it cannot be uttered. We just hurt on the inside for others.

**Romans 8:26-27: Likewise the Spirit also helpeth our infirmities: for we know not what we should pray for as we ought: but the Spirit itself maketh intercession for us with groanings which cannot be uttered. And he that searcheth the hearts knoweth what is the mind of the Spirit, because he maketh intercession for the saints according to the will of God.**

The Lord is searching for hearts that will intercede and He will use them many times to travail.

We also travail for our own infirmities (moral and physical weaknesses). Many people after receiving the Holy Spirit have a siege of crying and grieving. This is the Holy Spirit cleansing their spirits and souls with the water of tears. We are so full of the things of this world and the sins of the past that we need this cleansing. We should not resist this, but yield to it until all is washed away and we come into the place of joy and peace.

We haven't been taught much in this area, so many times the Lord tries to give us a burden for someone or something and we don't recognize it as such, but think that something is wrong with us. We pray to have a burden for lost souls and when we get one, we rebuke the Holy Spirit (thinking He is the enemy) because we do not understand the form of burden that travail takes. Often, we become depressed for no logical reason and, not recognizing it as travail, endure it or ignore it rather than praying until it lifts. The Lord tries to get us to pray; and when we do, not only does that depressed feeling leave, but we can break through spiritual barriers for someone else. The Lord also brings people to our hearts or our minds, and we need to be sensitive in the Spirit as to what the Lord speaks to us about them. They may be in need of prayer and the Spirit could be trying to get us to pray by bringing them to our remembrance. This is especially true if they remain in our thoughts for awhile. Praying in the Spirit like this is an invaluable tool.

We may have a burden for someone but not know his need. We should keep praying until we are released from that burden. Sometimes, we get the prayer victory in a matter of minutes; in other cases it may be longer. As we are led by the Spirit, He directs our prayer lives. He never puts a burden on us that is so heavy that we are unable to get freedom from it as we pray. The Lord knows we have earthly chores that must be attended to, so many times He gives us a burden that comes and goes so we can pray at those times when it is intense, and still attend to our earthly duties at other times. There is a time for travail, for work and for praise. The Spirit of God will balance us in all if we are sensitive to Him. **(Ecclesiastes 3:4, "A time to weep, and a time to laugh; a time to mourn, and a time to dance.")**

What is the purpose of travail? Travail produces spiritual children. **(Isaiah 66:8,"...for as soon as Zion travailed, she brought forth her children.")** Christians are spiritually referred to in the Word of God as Zion (God's people). As we travail, things are birthed in the Spirit. Many souls become "born again" through someone's travail. Things happen as we pray and travail.

Paul was a man who travailed. **(Galatians 4:19, "My little children, of whom I travail in birth again until Christ be formed in you.")** Paul had already travailed for them to be born into the kingdom of God, and now he was travailing for the remainder of the work to be done, Christ being formed in them. Paul knew that the destiny of baby Christians was to ultimately come into the fullness of Christ. Those little children were not to remain "babes," but were to be brought into maturity becoming sons of God. Travail produces sons.

Travail is also a form of suffering for Christ because we choose to endure the pain in our hearts in order that others may be set free. Our flesh suffers, yet it produces life in others. Paul was willing to do this for Christ. **(Colossians 1:24: Who now rejoice in my sufferings for you, and fill up that which is be-**

hind of the afflictions of Christ in my flesh for his body's sake, which is the church.)

There are many different forms that travail may take and varying depths of pain involved. Some of these are mild sensations of heaviness or depression, or just the general feeling of a burden. Some people weep, cry, moan or groan. Others even experience symptoms like birth pains or heart pains while in deep travail. One can experience any of these feelings separately or in combination.

Examples of these same experiences can be found in the lives of Bible saints. Daniel was a saint who experienced travail. In **Daniel 7:15**, he is seen grieving in the spirit. **I Daniel was grieved in my spirit in the midst of my body, and the visions of my head troubled me.** Also in **Daniel 8:27** and **Daniel 10:8**, we find him feeling faint, sick, and weak during the time he was in prayer. He was fine, though, after he finished praying. Hannah is another example of a travailing saint. We find her story in **1 Samuel 1:5-18**. It shows her weeping and in such agony that the priest accuses her of being drunk.

**1 Samuel 1:10: And she was in bitterness of soul, and prayed unto the Lord, and wept sore. Verses 13-15: Now Hannah, she spake in her heart; only her lips moved, but her voice was not heard: therefore Eli thought she had been drunken. And Eli said unto her, How long wilt thou be drunken? put away thy wine from thee. And Hannah answered and said, No, my lord, I am a woman of a sorrowful spirit: I have drunk neither wine nor strong drink, but have poured out my soul before the Lord.**

Hannah's travail produced a son in her life. Our travail will produce spiritual sons.

Most travailing is done privately because people who are not walking in the Spirit do not understand this type of prayer. As our understanding opens up to this truth in God's Word, more and more groups of believers will intercede with the spirit of travail upon them all, thus sharing the burden corporately.

The degrees and depths of travail span the mild forms to the very, very deep forms. One deep form incorporates the actual feeling of birth pains (the same pains that accompany the labor of a woman giving birth to a child). These "birth pains" are experienced by men as well as by women. (In the spirit there is neither male nor female.) **Galatians 3:28: There is neither Jew nor Greek, there is neither bond nor free, there is neither male nor female: for ye are all one in Christ Jesus.** We must have Scripture to support all spiritual experiences, so where is this to be found in the Word of God? In **Jeremiah 30:5-6**, we find an account of men travailing as women,

**For thus saith the Lord; We have heard a voice of trembling, of fear, and not of peace. Ask ye now, and see whether a man doth travail with child? wherefore do I see every man with his hands on his loins, as a woman in travail, and all faces are turned into paleness?** Here we find that after travail, they were released from their bonds, the yokes were taken off their necks and they were free to serve the Lord. Travail brought freedom to these men!

If we have a question as to whether it is the Lord presenting us with a burden that needs travailing prayer, or whether it is the enemy seeking to put depression on us, we can simply seek Him for the answer. Prayer is the way to rid ourselves of all kinds of depression. As we begin to pray, the Lord will show us if the depression is in us or if we are carrying a prayer burden for someone else. As we yield to God and resist the devil, we will get the victory.

One account that shows Jesus in travail is found in **John 11:32-44**. We are all familiar with this account of Jesus raising Lazarus from the dead. However, many of us have not noticed the travail that preceded this miracle. Beginning in verse 32, we read,

**Then when Mary was come where Jesus was, and saw him, she fell down at his feet, saying unto him, Lord, if thou hadst been here, my brother had not died. When Jesus there-**

fore saw her weeping, and the Jews also weeping which came with her, he groaned in the spirit, and was troubled, And said, Where have ye laid him? They said unto him, Lord, come and see. Jesus wept.

We see that the Lord had such a burden that He not only wept, but also groaned in the Spirit. He certainly was not crying because Lazarus was dead, for He knew that He was about to be brought back to life. He was crying in the Spirit, breaking the bonds of Satan, so that this miracle would come forth and bring life back to Lazarus. Verse 38 says,

Jesus therefore again groaning in himself cometh to the grave. It was a cave, and a stone lay upon it. Jesus said, Take ye away the stone. Martha, the sister of him that was dead, saith unto him, Lord, by this time he stinketh: for he hath been dead four days. Jesus saith unto her, Said I not unto thee, that, if thou wouldest believe, thou shouldest see the glory of God?

He was still in travail when he approached the grave. He then spoke the words for Lazarus to come forth, and the miracle took place as he was raised from the dead.

The greatest travail of all time was the Lord's travail of soul in the Garden of Gethsemane before He went to the cross for the sins of the world.

Luke 22:41-44: And he was withdrawn from them about a stone's cast, and kneeled down, and prayed, Saying, Father, if thou be willing, remove this cup from me: nevertheless not my will, but thine, be done. And there appeared an angel unto him from heaven, strengthening him. And being in agony he prayed more earnestly: and his sweat was as it were great drops of blood falling down to the ground.

This travail was so agonizing and painful that it caused Him to sweat blood. The Lord knew what awaited Him on the cross of Calvary. He could never have faced the crucifixion without first praying through and getting the victory in the spirit. This great travail gave Him the serenity and courage to face the traumatic events of the next day. He had won the victory in the spirit before He ever faced the enemy in the flesh.

We too can learn from this to fight our battles in the spirit. Then we will not have to resort to fleshly means of dealing with problems. Changes occur when we pray and travail. We find that when Zion travails, children are brought forth. The Lord wants us to take His burdens as our burdens. By doing this we are identifying with Him in His sufferings. **(2 Timothy 2:12, If we suffer, we shall also reign with him; if we deny him, he also will deny us.)** We know that as we are willing to suffer with Him and travail for others, we also will reign with Him, reaping the reward of joy by seeing the travail of our souls come forth even as Jesus did. **Isaiah 53:11-12: He shall see of the travail of his soul, and shall be satisfied: by his knowledge shall my righteous servant justify many; for he shall bear their iniquities. Therefore will I divide him a portion with the great, and he shall divide the spoil with the strong; because he hath poured out his soul unto death: and he was numbered with the transgressors; and he bare the sin of many, and made intercession for the transgressors.**

True intercessors will have the spirit of travail come upon them, for truly this is one of the keys that will bring the kingdom of God to the earth. The overcomers will be men and women who experience the same sorrows that our Lord experienced and who also will inherit the same things Jesus did.

**Revelation 21:4-7: And God shall wipe away all tears from their eyes; and there shall be no more death, neither sorrow, nor crying, neither shall there be any more pain: for the former things are passed away. And he that sat upon the throne said, Behold, I make all things new. And he said unto me, Write: for these words are true and faithful. And he said unto me, It is done. I am Alpha and Omega, the beginning and the end. I will give unto him that is athirst of the fountain of the water of life freely. He that overcometh shall inherit all things; and I will be his God, and he shall be my son.**

In **Ezekiel 9**, we see the Lord calls for a mark to be placed upon all who sigh and cry in prayer because they are burdened about the condition of God's people. These intercessors are given the "mark of God" and thus are protected when judgment comes upon sin. We too can experience deliverance as we cry and travail for others. Travailing prayer is a mighty weapon.

## Key of Fasting

Another key that nearly has been lost to the modern church, and one that some suppose was only for early day Christians, is the key of fasting. Looking closely at the Word of God, we see that the Lord never did away with the principle of fasting, but it has been man who has attempted to make it obsolete. Fasting is still a valid key that can be used today to bring us into kingdom living.

What is fasting? It is another means by which we can suffer for the Lord, through the voluntary abstinence from eating. Biblical fasting is to bring spiritual results and is not done simply for physical purposes.

Doctors today are discovering the physical benefits of this practice and have found that abstaining from food (not water) for several days has a wonderful cleansing effect upon the body. Many impurities are burned up within the body as it is denied food, thus clearing the mind, and cleansing and healing the body. Even nature shows us that fasting is good medicine as we automatically lose our appetites when sickness strikes. Many people in the world are practicing fasting and finding it not only healthful, but even a wonderful way to lose weight quickly. However, even though we may enjoy these benefits while fasting, the Christian primarily fasts for spiritual purposes and not for health reasons. Obeying spiritual principles can produce positive physical results, but they are added blessings. Even people that are underweight who fast for spiritual purposes have been known to gain weight after completing their fasts.

The Lord tells us in **Matthew 6:16-18** that when we fast, we are to do it unto the Lord. He doesn't say if we fast.

**Moreover when ye fast, be not, as the hypocrites, of a sad countenance: for they disfigure their faces, that they may appear unto men to fast. Verily I say unto you, They have their reward. But thou, when thou fastest, anoint thine head, and wash thy face; That thou appear not unto men to fast, but unto thy Father which is in secret: and thy Father, which seeth in secret, shall reward thee openly.** We can see that our motives in fasting must be pure. We are not to do it in order to broadcast it, but we are to do it as quietly and simply as possible so as not to attract attention to ourselves. We are to appear to others as though we are not fasting. There are exceptions, such as when we are fasting as a group for a specific thing. Then it must be announced so that others can take part. We find this in **Joel 1:14, Sanctify ye a fast, call a solemn assembly, gather the elders and all the inhabitants of the land into the house of the Lord your God, and cry unto the Lord.** The main thing the Lord desires is that it be done unto Him and not as a show unto men. Our heart attitude must be right to produce spiritual results.

Jesus, by fasting, set an example that we might follow in His steps. **Matthew 4:1-4: Then was Jesus led up of the Spirit into the wilderness to be tempted of the devil. And when he had fasted forty days and forty nights, he was afterward an hungred. And when the tempter came to him, he said, If thou be the Son of God, command that these stones be made bread. But he answered and said, It is written, Man shall not live by bread alone, but by every word that proceedeth out of the mouth of God.**

This Scripture shows us that the Lord drank water but did not eat food, for it says that after forty days he was hungry. The normal fast is without food, drinking water only.

There are also absolute fasts recorded in the Bible. Upon Saul's conversion in **Acts 9:9**, he immediately went on an absolute fast for three days, having neither food nor water. **(And he**

**was three days without sight, and neither did eat nor drink.)** The body can go for a number of days without food, but cannot go for long periods without water. Therefore, the Bible does not record any absolute fasts that go beyond three days, except the account of Moses spending forty days and nights on top of Mount Sinai (Horeb) without food or water.

**Exodus 34:28-29: And he was there with the Lord forty days and forty nights; he did neither eat bread, nor drink water. And he wrote upon the tables the words of the covenant, the ten commandments. And it came to pass, when Moses came down from mount Sinai with the two tables of testimony in Moses' hand, when he came down from the mount, that Moses wist not that the skin of his face shown while he talked with him.**

We can see that because Moses was in the literal presence of the Lord, it was that presence that sustained him so he neither needed food nor water. This, of course, is an exceptional fast.

The Lord did not set up any specific duration that we are to fast, but from His teachings, we see that he did expect us to fast.

**Luke 5:34-35: And he said unto them, Can ye make the children of the bridechamber fast, while the bridegroom is with them? But the days will come, when the bridegroom shall be taken away from them, and then shall they fast in those days**.

Fasting can be done for one meal, one day, one month or for however long God leads. It depends on how the Holy Spirit speaks to us. Shorter fasts are easier to endure until we have built up our "spiritual muscles." A helpful book we recommend is Arthur Wallis' "God's Chosen Fast." It is a spiritual and practical guide to fasting. A three day fast is most beneficial as a spiritual cleansing. An example of this is Paul's being thrust into his fast upon conversion. After the three days of cleansing, he received the Holy Spirit and his eyesight when Ananias laid hands on him (**Acts 9:17-18**). We also can be spiritually cleansed by fasting so that we receive more of the Lord's Spirit and have our spiritual eyes opened to new dimensions. A three day fast is also especially helpful in breaking any addictive habits.

These then are two reasons for fasting: We receive spiritual cleansing and our spiritual eyes are opened, and we also obtain victory over the devil. When Jesus encountered Satan, He was able to overcome Him because His fasting had given Him spiritual strength. **Isaiah 58:6** also gives us light on this purpose of fasting: **Is not this the fast that I have chosen? to loose the bands of wickedness, to undo the heavy burdens, and to let the oppressed go free, and that ye break every yoke?** Many people believe that fasting is to move the hand of God, when in actuality it is to make Satan turn loose of the things he is holding.

Fasting looses the bands of wickedness. When Jesus discussed the keys to the kingdom, He told us to bind and loose. When we fast, we loose the bands of wickedness, undo the heavy burdens, set the oppressed free, and break every yoke of the enemy. Fasting is an important key to getting the victory over hard situations that do not seem to respond to normal prayer.

Fasting builds our faith. In fact, this is what Jesus meant when he spoke to the disciples in **Matthew 17:21** in answer to why they were not able to cast a demon out of a child. He said, **Howbeit this kind goeth not out but by prayer and fasting.** He was telling them if they wanted their faith to be at such a level as to be able to cast out demons, then they must fast and pray for their faith to increase.

Fasting also makes it easier for us to hear the voice of the Lord. We find an account of this in **Acts 13:2-3.**

**As they ministered to the Lord, and fasted, the Holy Ghost said, Separate me Barnabas and Saul for the work whereunto I have called them. And when they had fasted and prayed, and laid their hands on them, they sent them away.**

While fasting, the Holy Spirit spoke to them and gave them direction. We too can be directed by the Lord if we seek Him through prayer and fasting.

Fasting and mourning are closely associated in the Bible. Two examples of this are found in Ezra and Nehemiah.

**Ezra 10:6: Then Ezra rose up from before the house of God, and went into the chamber of Johanan the son of Eliashib: and when he came thither, he did eat no bread, nor drink water: for he mourned because of the transgression of them that had been carried away. Nehemiah 1:4: And it came to pass, when I heard these words, that I sat down and wept, and mourned certain days, and fasted, and prayed before the God of heaven.**

From these Scriptures, we see that fasting and travail were combined. Both of these men were fasting for the repentance of God's people. How we need this same kind of intercession today. Here were men so burdened for the sins of their people that they fasted, travailed and prayed.

Today, God is looking for people who are willing to take the same kind of burdens in the Spirit. After being filled with the Holy Spirit, so many are eager to do something for the Lord; however, due to a lack of proper teaching, they end up doing works in the flesh instead of works in the Spirit. Works that we do in our own strength profit nothing, but works that are inspired by the Spirit are profitable and bring results. Prayer is work in the Spirit. That is why it is not easy to pray. Travail and fasting are works in the Spirit. Witnessing under God's leadership is a spiritual work. God is looking for laborers who are ready to go to work for Him. **(Matthew 9:37-38: Then saith he unto his disciples, The harvest truly is plenteous, but the labourers are few; Pray ye therefore the Lord of the harvest, that he will send forth labourers into his harvest.)** The Lord is looking for workers, people who will labor to produce eternal results. Laboring in the Spirit brings many into the kingdom of God and causes much growth in the church.

Fasting is also one of these labors. It is a form of afflicting our soul. **(Isaiah 58:3: Wherefore have we fasted, say they, and thou seest not? wherefore have we afflicted our soul, and**

**thou takest no knowledge?...)** By afflicting our soul, we say to our flesh, "Flesh, you are demanding to eat, but Christ is stronger than the desires of my soul. My spirit shall rule my soul, and my soul shall not have dominion over me."

Numerous individuals today are in bondage to their appetites because they have never denied themselves anything. The Lord wants us to be ruled by the Spirit, not by the flesh. Fasting brings the flesh unto subjection of the Spirit. **(Matthew 4:4: But he answered and said, It is written, Man shall not live by bread alone, but by every word that proceedeth out of the mouth of God.)**

Fasting is also a way we can minister unto the Lord. We read in **Acts 13:2** that they ministered unto the Lord and fasted. It is a way we can offer the time we generally spend in eating as unto the Lord in prayer. As we spend this time with Him, it causes things to happen in the Spirit.

We do not understand this principle any more than other mysteries in the Bible, but we find that by applying it we get results. There are many things I don't understand with my natural mind, but I receive them by faith because the Word of God says they are true. If God's Word says it, that settles it. I don't even understand why Jesus had to die on a cross to save us from our sins. However, because I believed that He did and received His forgiveness in my heart, I was "born again." Likewise, I do not understand all the principles of fasting, but I do know they work.

We have discussed the absolute and the normal fasts, but we need to also mention the partial fast. This is a fast where we restrict our intake of food, but do not totally abstain.

We have a record of this in **Daniel 10:2-3, In those days I Daniel was mourning three full weeks. I ate no pleasant bread, neither came flesh nor wine in my mouth, neither did I anoint myself at all, till three whole weeks were fulfilled**.

Daniel went on a three-week partial fast, restricting his diet of all pleasant food, meat and wine. It was during this time that he had a visitation from an angel. Fasting always suppresses the flesh and heightens our spiritual sensitivity. Generally speaking, we hear the Lord's voice more easily while fasting.

We all can benefit by giving up our pleasant bread for a season. The Lord blesses us for whatever sacrifices we make for Him. Our country is suffering under a spirit of gluttony and it would be a great blessing for the United States to have a time of national fasting unto God. We sit down and eat many times when we are not even hungry, simply because it is a habit. We should not eat out of habit or tradition, but rather that we might glorify Christ in our bodies. **(1 Corinthians 10:31: Whether therefore ye eat, or drink, or whatsoever ye do, do all to the glory of God.)**

Fasting sometimes comes spontaneously. Often if people are grieving they lose their appetites and unconsciously fast. That is why mourning and fasting are mentioned together in the Bible. Another type of spontaneous fasting occurs when we are so busy seeking God about a situation or a spiritual goal that we simply forget to eat. (We are moving too fast to take time to eat because we are concentrating on the things of the Spirit. We are moving in the spirit in a "fast" way. The fasting acts as spiritual dynamite to speed things up in the Spirit that would normally take a longer time to come to pass.) Some Christians are forced to fast due to a lack of food in their part of the world. They can dedicate this time to God and He will bless it as He would a voluntary fast.

Does fasting move the hand of God? No. If we believe that God withholds from us and we have to fight to get Him to bless us, then we have a wrong conception of the Lord. **Isaiah 58:6** indicates that fasting is not to move the hand of the Lord, but it is to make Satan turn loose of what he is holding back that rightfully belongs to us. Jesus died so we could have the blessings. They belong to us as His children. However, we must press in and de-mand the enemy to release some things. This is our right as sons of God. Sometimes Satan still controls much territory in our lives and the lives of our loved ones. He has many in bondage. Fasting is a key that breaks loose the bands of wickedness. As we fast and pray, Satan must let our children who are bound by spirits of rebellion and drugs go free. He must take his hands off our loved ones, our friends and family. Some people are so bound that only fasting can loose them from the wicked chains of darkness.

We need to be sensitive to the Holy Spirit as to when fasting is needed. Sometimes it is not necessary because the problem has already been "prayed through." We need simply to rest in the Lord until His time for our answer to arrive. If we fast at those times, we will just be going hungry. We need also to seek the Lord as to whether He would have us go on a partial fast, normal fast or total fast. If we will ask, He will let us know. He will confirm His will to us. If we cannot hear His voice too clearly, He will send somebody to speak His counsel to us. We must trust Him.

We need also to check our motives when we fast. If they are selfish, our fast will not be accepted by the Lord. We see this in **Jeremiah 14:10 and 12,**

**Thus saith the Lord unto this people, Thus have they loved to wander, they have not refrained their feet, therefore the Lord doth not accept them; he will now remember their iniquity, and visit their sins. When they fast, I will not hear their cry; and when they offer burnt offering and an oblation, I will not accept them: but I will consume them by the sword, and by the famine, and by the pestilence.** We cannot fast and have evil, unrepented sin or selfishness in our lives and expect God to answer our prayers. Many times we don't even recognize selfish prayers. When we pray for our loved ones to be saved or delivered, and our motive is to bring relief to ourselves instead of being concerned that they receive the peace and joy of Jesus, we are wrong. Let us examine our hearts when we seek God for anything.

**Isaiah 58** is the great fasting chapter. Here we read how this key can break the bonds of wickedness, undo the heavy burdens and bring healing. It frees the oppressed and the depressed. It breaks every yoke. Some people are yoked to bad habits in this world, and fasting can break those yokes so they can be free to enter into the kingdom of God. A three-day fast will break most addictions.

**Isaiah 58:7** also says, **Is it not to deal thy bread to the hungry, and that thou bring the poor that are cast out to thy house?** Fasting makes it possible for us not only to give "spiritual bread" to those that are hungry, but also releases our finances so that we can give "natural bread" to the poor and needy. The Lord wants us to have an abundance so we can be a blessing to others. He will bring the poor to our houses to be fed. He wants us to be able to minister to others. He will give us a ministry and cause people to be drawn to our doorstep by the Holy Spirit for counsel and prayer.

**Verse 7** continues, **when thou seest the naked, that thou cover him.** We are to cover others' sin through fasting and prayers of mercy. We are to ask God to forgive them and give them another chance. If we were stripped naked right now and our lives were bared before the world, every one of us would be ashamed and embarrassed about our past sins. None of us could stand. All of us would fall down naked, exposed and humiliated. However, we do not have to suffer this because Jesus paid the price for our sins and washed those things away. Praise God! They are not there anymore; God does not remember them, and neither should we. **(Hebrews 10:17: And their sins and iniquities will I remember no more.)** We need to pray for others to be released from the burden of sin that is upon their lives.

**Verse 7** also says, **...and that thou hide not thyself from thine own flesh?** One trick of the enemy is to get us so busy ministering to others that we fail to minister to our own flesh. We must also ask the Lord to do a work of cleansing in our lives, and also make sure that we take time to let the Lord minister to us through His word, and in time spent alone with Him. Also, we are not to neglect our own flesh and blood. We must not get so busy with others' needs that we do not minister to our own families. We are to fast for them, pray for them and spend time with them.

In **verse 8** we see the fruits of fasting, **Then shall thy light** break forth as the morning, and thine health shall spring forth speedily: and thy righteousness shall go before thee; the glory of the Lord shall be thy reward. Healing will come forth quickly through fasting. If we have a besetting sin that we cannot get the victory over, fasting will strengthen us spiritually and deliver us from that bondage so that our righteousness can go before us. (What a beautiful promise that the glory of the Lord shall be our reward. We receive a reward during the time of fasting, but it does not stop there. We also will be rewarded by seeing things come forth in the future as answers to our prayers.)

Verse 9 says, Then shalt thou call, and the Lord shall answer; thou shalt cry, and he shall say, Here I am. If thou take away from the midst of thee the yoke, the putting forth of the finger, and speaking vanity. By this we see there are conditions to our fast. We cannot point our fingers at others in condemnation if we expect our prayers to be answered. We must come humbly before the Lord if we desire to see our prayers answered.

The remainder of **Isaiah 58** explains that the Lord will cause us to be lights to others, and that we shall not walk in darkness but have the Lord continually guiding us. He says we shall be taken care of in drought. No matter what is happening in the land, we shall have plenty. Waste places shall be rebuilt, and the Lord will restore and repair the damage that has been done to our lives. We shall ride upon the high places of the earth and shall inherit God's blessings. Fasting brings restoration in our individual lives.

## Restoration of the Church

We are living in the time of restoration of the church now. God has begun a work of restoration in us. The power of the Holy Spirit is being restored to the church. God is healing His people and giving back to them the things Satan has robbed. The Lord is restoring truth to the church again, so she can rise from obscurity and be seen in love and power, even as she was in New Testament days.

The world is looking for a church that has the power to heal and bless, a church that walks in victory. The world wants to see a church that is not hypocritical, a church that is holy and full of love. We are the individual members of that church if we are born again. The work must begin in us personally before it can manifest itself corporately. The Lord is returning for a bride without spot or blemish. God is preparing her. We must have the keys to the kingdom so that we can come to that place in God where the world can tell the difference between "us" and "them."

Fasting is a wonderful tool given to help bring us to that place. God's ultimate desire is that we live "fasted" lives, thus reducing the need for periodic fasting. However, until we come to the place where the kingdom of God means more to us than food, we need to set our wills to fast in order to bring our bodies under subjection to the Spirit of the Lord.

Paul was an overcomer and says in **I Corinthians 9:27, But I keep under my body, and bring it into subjection: lest that by any means, when I have preached to others, I myself should be a castaway.** For us to overcome we must do likewise. To grow in God we must follow the methods He mapped out in His Word. The Lord is encouraging us to walk in His footsteps so that we might attain the same victory that Paul did. It is not impossible; we just have not understood God's ultimate purpose for our lives; we have lived far below the level God intended. Even though we will walk through some hard places in this life, we will be able to say it was worth it all when we come into the same perfection that Paul did. **II Corinthians 11:27: In weariness and painfulness, in watchings often, in hunger and thirst, in fastings often, in cold and nakedness. Philippians 3:8: Yea doubtless, and I count all things but loss for the excellency of the knowledge of Christ Jesus my Lord: for whom I have suffered the loss of all things, and do count them but dung, that I may win Christ.**

The keys of prayer, praise, worship, intercession, travail and fasting will bring us to the same place that Paul attained through Jesus. We can have a similar anointing in our lives, perform like miracles as Paul performed, and we too can achieve the same victories in the name of Jesus. We can enter into such a dimension of spiritual warfare that the demons and devils obey us. Although spiritual warfare is another key to the kingdom, we will not deal with it here. We can expose Satan's devices and learn the ways by which we overcome him. These important keys will unlock many from the chains of darkness. Let us use all the keys to the kingdom so that the kingdom of God might be formed in us.

"Father, You know each one that is reading this book today, and I ask You to reach out and meet their needs. Lord, minister to their need now through the power of the Holy Spirit. If there are those who have not been filled with Your Spirit, I pray that You would fill them now to overflowing. Give them their heavenly language with which to praise and worship You. Lord, to those who need You as Savior, touch them and come into their hearts; may they be born again and placed into Your kingdom. For those who need healing in their bodies, touch them with Your creative power. Father, deliver and set free those who are suffering from depression and are bound by the things of this world. Bless Your people, Lord, as they seek Your will and way for their lives. Give them Your strength to use the keys of the kingdom to overcome the enemy. In Jesus' name, Amen."

# Index

**F**

Fasting 35, 36, 37, 38, 39, 40, 41, 42, 43, 44, 45, 46

**P**

Praise, a key to the Kingdom   1, 22, 23, 24, 25, 26, 27, 46
Praise brings healing to our souls and bodies 25
Praise in everything 22
Praise overcomes Satan 22, 24, 26, 27
Praise through singing 25, 26
Prayer   1, 3, 4, 5, 6, 7, 8, 9, 10, 11, 12, 13, 14, 15, 19, 27, 28, 29, 30, 31, 32, 33, 34 35, 39, 40, 44, 46
Prayer, forms of:
  Anointing with oil 6
  Binding and loosing 2, 7, 8, 38
  Intercessory prayer 1, 12, 13, 14, 15, 19, 20, 29, 31, 34, 35, 39, 46
  Laying on of hands 6, 17
  Lord's Prayer 10, 11, 22
  Persevering 9
  Prayer of agreement 7 8
  Praying in the Spirit 10, 15, 16, 17, 18, 19, 20, 21, 22, 27, 28, 30, 31, 33
  Should be directed to the Father 8

With uplifted hands  6
Without ceasing  9, 22

**T**

Travail   1, 27, 28, 29, 30, 31, 32, 33, 34, 35,
  39, 46

Additional Books by the Author:

Book Titles in the OVERCOMING LIFE SERIES:

PROVE ALL THINGS
THE TRUE GOD
THE WILL OF GOD
KEYS TO THE KINGDOM
EXPOSING SATAN'S DEVICES
HEALING OF THE SPIRIT, SOUL & BODY
NEITHER MALE NOR FEMALE
EXTREMES OR BALANCE?
THE PATHWAY INTO THE OVERCOMER'S WALK

Book Titles in the END TIMES SERIES:

MARK OF GOD OR MARK OF THE BEAST
PERSONAL SPIRITUAL WARFARE

For online orders, please visit our website

http://www.BibleResources.org

Christ Unlimited Ministries, Inc.
P.O. Box 850
Dewey, AZ 86327
U.S.A.

# Postnote

The Millers are very glad to receive mail from their readers; however, they are unable to answer the letters personally due the volume of mail that they receive. They will be happy to pray along with their intercessors for all who write with a prayer request; although they do no outside counseling as they believe this should be directed to local pastors as outlined in Scripture.

Christ Unlimited Ministries, Inc. is a non-profit church 501(c) (3) corporation. All contributions are tax deductible. We appreciate your prayers, encouragement and support. Your purchase of this book makes it possible for us to share free copies of Bibles, teaching literature, tracts and downloadable audio/video materials with ministers in third world countries who would otherwise not be able to purchase them.

**The Lord gave the word: great was the company of those that published it (Psalm 68:11).**

# For Additional Study

This book is taken from a course of Bible studies called the Overcoming Life Series. The entire series is a virtual "spiritual tool chest," as it covers a multitude of subjects every Christian faces in his walk with God. It also answers questions that many believers have concerning the current move of God. These are dealt with in a balanced approach and in the light of the Scripture. God's people are not to live frustrated, defeated lives, but rather they are to be victorious overcomers! Other books available with their companion workbooks are:

**PROVE ALL THINGS** - Christ warned that great deception would be one of the signs of the end times. In this book, instruction is given on how to recognize false prophets and teachings. Clear Scriptural guidelines are given on discerning the Spirit of truth versus the spirit of error. The book deals with how to judge without being judgmental.

**THE TRUE GOD** - This is a teaching on the character of God, explaining why God does certain things, and why it is against His nature to do other things. It differentiates between the things for which God is responsible and the things for which the devil is responsible. Our responsibility as Christians destined to overcome is made clear so that we can live victorious lives.

**THE WILL OF GOD** - This lesson teaches us not only how to know the will of God in our personal lives, family, ministry and finances, but also brings understanding as to why God allows sin, sickness and suffering in the world. As overcomers, Christians are not to suffer under many of the things we have accepted as normal.

**KEYS TO THE KINGDOM** - Instruction on how to gain authority in God's Kingdom through prayer is the topic of this book. Many principles and methods of prayer are covered, such as praying in the Spirit, fasting and prayer, travailing prayer, praise, intercession and spiritual warfare.

**EXPOSING SATAN'S DEVICES** - This book is a powerful expose' of Satan's tricks, tactics and lies. Cult and Occultic methods and groups are listed so Christians can detect their activity. Demon activity is discussed and deliverance and casting out demons is dealt with in detail. Satan's kingdom is uncovered and the Christian is taught to overcome through spiritual discernment and warfare.

**HEALING OF THE SPIRIT, SOUL AND BODY** - This book teaches how to overcome emotional problems, as well as physical ones, and how to receive divine healing. It also teaches how to renew the carnal mind and walk in the spirit of life, thereby overcoming depression, loneliness and fear.

**NEITHER MALE NOR FEMALE** - What is the woman's role in the church and home? Who is a woman's spiritual head and covering? Does God call women to the five-fold ministry? What does God's Word say about divorce, celibacy and choosing a marriage partner? These and other woman related topics are Scripturally examined.

**EXTREMES OR BALANCE?** - Many Christians have hurt the cause of Christ through "out-of-balance" teachings and demonstrations. This book shows how to avoid those areas. It also deals wisely with the excesses and extremes in the body of Christ.

**THE PATHWAY INTO THE OVERCOMER'S WALK** - This book contains answers to the questions an overcomer faces as he presses toward the prize of the high calling in Christ Jesus. How can we be conformed to the image of Christ? How does the Holy Spirit work with the overcomers in the end times? What are the overcomer's rewards?

**PERSONAL SPIRITUAL WARFARE** - Explains the invisible world of spiritual forces that influence our lives and how good can prevail over the evil around us as we prepare for the new kingdom age that is coming. This book will help you overcome problems in your finances, marriage, the emotional pressures of fear, anger and hurt. Here are the keys to victory through spiritual warfare.

**MARK OF GOD OR MARK OF THE BEAST** - Much has been written and said about the mark of the beast, but little has been said about the mark of God. What does the 666 mean and what is this mysterious mark? How is it linked to the world of finance? Has this mark already begun? This book answers many questions about the mark of the beast and the mark of God, and how they affect Christians.

Please visit our website for information on how to order the complete "Overcoming Life Bible Study." The website site is also an excellent source for additional books and Bible resources.

www.BibleResources.org

# Purpose and Vision

Go ye therefore, and teach all nations, baptiz-
ing them in the name of the Father, and of the Son,
and of the Holy Ghost: Teaching them to observe
all things whatsoever I have commanded you: and,
lo, I am with you alway, even unto the end of the
world. Amen.

Matthew 28:19,20

Christ Unlimited is not "another denomination," sect, or just
a separate group. It is an arm of the Body of Christ — the Church
of Jesus Christ, which has been called to strengthen the Body at
large. We also believe we have been called to help establish the
Kingdom of God in the earth.

Christ Unlimited is involved with all Bible-believing Christians regardless of their church or denominational affiliations and
committed to helping wherever possible in evangelistic and teaching outreaches.

Christ Unlimited believes that time is running out and the
Gospel has not been preached to every creature. Many nations
have not heard the Gospel, and in many places, doors for evange-
lism are closing. We believe it is time all Christians cooperated
with the Lord in breaking down denominational walls for a united
front line against the kingdom of darkness and in setting up the
Kingdom of the Lord Jesus Christ by the power of the Holy Spirit.

Christ Unlimited provides such tools as to enable the saints
of God to establish the Kingdom of God in the earth. We encour-
age groups of prayer warriors who will pray, fast, and intercede
for the nations. This, we believe, is weapon number one. We teach
believers how to overcome through spiritual warfare and through

knowing how to use their authority in Christ Jesus through the Word and the power of the Holy Spirit.

Christians need to know how to bring down the forces of darkness in their own lives and in the lives of those to whom they minister. We provide such tools as Bibles, literature, Christ Unlimited books, and an online prayer ministry. We publish the Gospel going out via any means of communication, including the internet, videos, as well as literature. We have teaching seminars, Bible schools, and correspondence courses, all aimed at winning souls to Christ and building the Body of Christ into maturity.

Bud and Betty Miller serve the Lord together as founders of the multi-visioned ministry outreach, Christ Unlimited. The outreaches of this ministry have stemmed from a tremendous desire to see the Word of God taught in its balanced entirety. The Millers are firm believers in prayer and, through prayer, have seen many released from the bondages of fear, failure, and defeat.

The outreaches of Christ Unlimited are in obedience to the words of our Lord in **Mark 16:15**: **Go ye into all the world and preach the gospel to every creature.** This mandate from the Lord presents a challenge to our generation as an estimated 25 percent of the world's population still have not heard the Good News of Jesus Christ.

Christ Unlimited Ministries also is dedicated to teaching God's Word. **Hosea 4:6** says: **My people are destroyed for lack of knowledge.** Many Christians are leading defeated lives simply because they do not know God's Word in its fullest.

Christ Unlimited Ministries has provided for those who desire to know God's Word in a greater way. The main thrust of the teaching and literature is directed at "How to be an overcomer." In the endtimes, we must be prepared to overcome the onslaughts of Satan. Many Christians are suffering needlessly, because they do not know how to overcome sickness, depression, divorce, fear, and financial failure. Christ Unlimited Ministries provides answers for troubled families as well as trains workers for service.

www.ingramcontent.com/pod-product-compliance
Lightning Source LLC
Chambersburg PA
CBHW020951030426
42339CB00004B/53